Creating Consistent Cash Flow

By

Christian Life Coach
Angela Showers

Showers Ink

Introduction

As a business owner I have witness several businesses open and close like revolving doors. After being in business for myself a few years, I realized how important it is to revamp your business. Revamping your business is as important as updating your computer software. If you get stuck doing the same routine you will continue to get the same results.

In this EBook I will give you 10 valuable tips that I have learned along the way. These tips have enhanced my skills, increased my business sales, and have given me massive exposure. If you are reading this EBook, it means that you are ready and willing to explore a new journey in your business adventure. The only way to get the results you are looking to receive is to simply take these tips and put them into action!

I have one word when it comes to revamping your business and that is to be **Flawless**!

Forever
Learning
About
Ways to
Lead
Elevate
Sale and
Satisfy

Unlimited Blessings,

Angela Showers

I want to see you succeed in business.

As a small business owner, every quarter I re-evaluate where I am in business. Every New Year it is a MUST to have already prepared your New Year business goals before December 25th. Every small business owner should take a look at their successes, failures, and new things they can do to help their business thrive in this New Year ahead.

 It has been a great challenge for many small business owners in this economy for the past years. However, every year gives you the opportunity to **revamp** your mission and refresh your procedures. Now is the time to re-evaluate your business and decide which new goals you should set in order to strengthen your operations and become more **profitable** for you and your business.

Like most of us, I'm sure you're tired of hearing and/or dealing with the economy. It's no secret that overall, things have taken a spiral nosedive. However, you have two options at this point, you can keep whining and do nothing or you can start thinking creatively and make things happen. The economy is not just affecting your business or small businesses, many big corporations have to regroup and revamp their business strategies as well.

Showers Ink

Here is some **Tips to Revamp Your Business** to ensure a **Consistence Cash Flow** in order to have your best years yet!

Tip #1

It may be time to rethink your customer base.

Ask yourself: What is my current customer semographic and how can I revamp my brand to appeal to customers outside my niche demographic to make up for less business by existing customers?

Sometimes it could be as simple as just rephrasing your marketing to appeal to a wider customer base, versus introducing new gadgets or product lines (which can be expensive and risky). Be wise and be honest to yourself and your business budget.

Showers Ink

Tip # 2

Technology is a wonderful thing, embrace it.

Technology has grown in so many ways throughout the years. All we have to do is take the time to learn how to use technology to benefit our business.

Ask yourself: How many times have you signed in on Facebook, Twitter, Myspace, Ning, or any other Social Network without advertising your business?

There are many ways to expose your business to the world; however you have to be willing to utilize technology for what it was created for. The great thing about that... It's Free!

In order to grow your business, you have to stay on top of what's new and working now. Go to your favorite search engine and look for some tele-seminars, webinars and workshops. Maybe even try reading a book. There is tons of information available out there and you'd be surprised at how much of it is actually FREE.

Showers Ink

Tip #3

Forget about the economy.

Don't get caught up with all of the negativity floating around about the economy. Success is a state of mind. Pay attention to how it changes your prospect's buying behavior, and come up with a creative way to market your products and or services to your clients. However, it is very important to value yourself and your services and or products.

Look around your office to see if there are areas you can afford to cut back on spending while also putting out great quality of services. See if there are any wasteful habits that you and staff may be doing when it comes to office supplies and products.

I have learned over the years that people will spend their money on what they feel is important and valuable to them. So make sure what you have to offer is being displayed and at its highest level of presentation.

Showers Ink

Tip #4

Build Value.

The days of the pushy salesperson or the door to door salesperson are HISTORY. People these days don't have as much extra cash or time as they used to and to be honest neither do you. So therefore, people expect great value for their time and their money.

I strongly advise that you focus less on selling your products and services and more on how you can improve or customize your services for each individual customer.

Rule #1 when it comes to building value is to remain professional at all times. Never, I repeat Never discuss personal business with employees or customers, this cuts down on people crossing your personal boundaries. Follow these tips and you'll definitely see the results.

Showers Ink

Tip #5

Develop a Plan.

So many business owners have spent most of their time as an entrepreneur winging it. I encourage you to sit down, set goals for both business and personal, and be sure to put them in writing. Whether this is your first time to setting goals or you are revisiting goals, put them in writing. Not only will this help you evaluate how well you did with goal setting, you can keep track of each goal and mark it off your list. Written goals can also identify areas that failed and provide opportunities for change.

Your current policies and procedures should also be reviewed and if you don't have any written policies, now is a good time to begin writing some. Do you have an employee handbook? If not, set a goal to write one.

By putting goals in writing, it will give you a better opportunity to determine what works and what isn't working as well as increasing sales revenues and profits.

My favorite saying is "Lack of planning is a plan to fail." Set the goals for your business and make it happen.

Showers Ink

Tip # 6

Amp up customer service

With the economy the way it is, it's easy to become too focused on the internal operations. However, it's your customers that make your business, and you need to remind them that they come first.

"Set your company aside from others by offering the best customer service possible." Return every phone call within a day and be on time for all of your appointments. That alone will separate you from your competition. Also, I would suggest putting up a privacy customer comment box. This will give you the opportunity to get feedback from your clients/customers.

Don't always assume that you are doing great in the customer service department because what you consider great customer service could be different for your customers stand point. Creating customer service surveys give you the opportunity to see what each customer is looking for when they come in contact with business like yours.

Showers Ink

Tip # 7

Budgeting Expenses

Take a long hard look at what your current expenses are. Can you identify areas that are excessive or non-essential? Start with your Income Statement where you can quickly identify sales, cost of sales, and net profits.

What expenses seem high to you and what areas can you afford to cut? Telephone and utilities are often big expenses for businesses, so go with only services you need instead of those that are not needed . Do you just settle for what the utility companies offer or have you visited your local utility companies and asked about discounts or programs to help you save money? If not, this is the time to do it.

Take a long look at all of your expenses and see which ones should be decreased, stay the same, or changed. Even with your office supplies, what can be omitted from your list and what can be recycled and used for multiple purposes?

Showers Ink

Tip #8

Host an Event

 If you don't want to do the footwork to market your business, bring the customers/clients to you. Hosting an event doesn't have to cost an arm and a leg, the biggest investment will be your time.

Free or low cost events, workshops, and seminars are a great way to get your ideal prospects in front of you.

Another great idea would be to collaborate with another business owner that has the same target market as you but offers a different product or service of course.

Collaborating makes it less of a strain on finances and time because you can split the cost and the planning of the event and it also builds a great Business-2-Business relationship!

Showers Ink

Tip # 9

Do Some Speaking

 Speaking is another great way to get you and your company's name out there in the public's eye. You can brand yourself and your company by educating the community on specific topics that your company addresses.

Do not expect to get paid right away, you will have to do some free speaking engagements at first but not to worry because it's helping you build your brand so in the long run, it will definitely pay off.

Do as much research as possible on the topics that coordinate with your business so you can deliver as many unfamiliar facts as possible to your audience. Most of all relax and have fun while doing it!

Showers Ink

Tip #10

Set Lifestyle Goals

As a small business owner we work longer hours than people who don't own their own company. Ask yourself: How much time are you spending and is your lifestyle suffering? Ask your family about how much you work and things you can do to improve your family life.

Some small business owners feel their company will fall apart unless they are on-site constantly. If this is you, you aren't putting much trust in your staff (if you have a staff). If you trust your staff, consider shortening your hours to help meet family commitments.

When preparing your business goals (or any goals), set aside time to do it well. Ask employees (if you have any) for their input on what could be changed. Make an appointment with your accountant (if you have one) to help you identify expense areas that could be cut. Consider changing your advertising if your old campaign didn't or doesn't work. Failing to set goals each year can make your business suffer and in today's economy. We need you to stay on top.

Showers Ink

Self Business Coaching Journal

Who are your current customers?

Showers Ink

Describe your idea target clients?

Showers Ink

List 5 problems that your client can solve for your clients. How?

Showers Ink

What's the biggest problem your business can solve for your clients?

Showers Ink

What are 5 unique advantages for using your company's services?

Showers Ink

What would be the greatest advantage of a customer using your services?

Showers Ink

What are all the ways a customer can contact you?

Showers Ink

What makes the most strategic sense as a person's 1st point of contact with your business? Why?

Showers Ink

What is your most effective marketing strategy?

Showers Ink

What is your least effective marketing tool? Why?

Showers Ink

What sets you apart from your competitors?

Showers Ink

List 5 things you need to do in order to improve your business.

Showers Ink

Biblical Scriptures for Small Business

Showers Ink

Scriptures for Encouragement

Deuteronomy 8:18 NIV

But remember the LORD your God, for it is he who gives you the ability to produce wealth, and so confirms his covenant, which he swore to your ancestors, as it is today. All of our skills and special talents that we use in our businesses are all given to us by God. He gives us the ability to make money and cut deals. He did it for our parents and mentors and he does it for us too.

Romans 12:2 NIV

Do not conform to the pattern of this world, but be transformed by the renewing of your mind. Then you will be able to test and approve what God's will is–his good, pleasing and perfect will. The bible commands us to be innovative in our businesses. We should not ever try to be like anyone else. The world is still waiting on a better mousetrap, and we should never rest on our successes. We must renew ourselves by being lifelong learners and reading constantly.

I Thessalonians 5:16-19 NIV

Be joyful always; pray continually; give thanks in all circumstances; this is the will of God for your life. It is important to have a prayerful life as an entrepreneur; it will help you on those days when things do not go your way. You need to have the strength to thank God, even when you do not win that big contract. God protects us when we do not get opportunities that we think we can't survive without. Always be grateful.

Showers Ink

Proverbs 16:18 NIV

Pride goes before destruction, a haughty spirit before a fall. Many entrepreneurs struggle with pride. Do not be afraid to tell clients or employees that you do not know the answer. Try to diffuse any issues with truth and by taking full responsibility for fixing the problem. Never let your ego get in the way of doing what's in the best interest of your business.

II Corinthians 9:8 NIV

And God is able to bless you abundantly, so that in all things at all times, having all that you need, you will abound in every good work. God always delivers to us what we need in order to do our best work. Sometimes he sends a check we need just in time, and other times he sends us creativity to find the best solution to our challenges. Trust in the Lord at all times.

II Timothy 1:7 NIV

For the Spirit God gave us does not make us timid, but gives us power, love and self-discipline. Fear is the enemy of entrepreneurship. God wants us to go out with the power he gives us to pursue our ideas in business.

Hebrews 12:11 NIV

No discipline seems pleasant at the time, but painful. Later on, however, it produces a harvest of righteousness and peace for those who have been trained by it. You must be fiscally disciplined in business. You cannot put all your hard work at risk by not being focused on your big picture goals and your monthly sales goals. It is painful at times, but it will produce quite a harvest.

Showers Ink

I Corinthians 9:24 NIV

Do you not know that in a race all the runners run, but only one gets the prize? Run in such a way as to get the prize. Running a business is hard. It's a marathon not a sprint. There will be plenty of stumbling blocks in your way. Everyone trips and falls while running this race, but winners get up faster than everyone else. You must do what you need to do to win your race.

Mark 5:36 NIV

Overhearing what they said, Jesus told them, "Don't be afraid; just believe." There will be times when you are the only person who believes in your business dream. Don't be afraid. Believe in yourself and your business idea.

Ecclesiastes 11:4 AMP

He who observes the wind [and waits for all conditions to be favorable] will not sow, and he who regards the clouds will not reap. You must be willing to make decisions in your small business. No one is going to come along and do it for you. Make hard decisions quickly, so you can move on to doing the work needed to help your customers.

Proverbs 11:14 NIRV

Without the guidance of good leaders a nation falls. But many good advisers can save it. It is critical to have a kitchen cabinet of advisors for your small business. Your business will not survive on your experience alone. Pull together four to five people who are invested in your success. The group should include an existing entrepreneur, a customer, a mentor, a lawyer and a accountant. Seek out a mastermind group or peer to peer mentoring program to help as well.

Showers Ink

Philippians 4:13 NKJV
I can do all things through Christ who strengthens me.
Whenever you struggle with your self-confidence read this
bible verse to yourself. There will be times in your
business when you need to force yourself to stretch beyond
what you think is possible. You can do it. I believe in you.
Jeremiah 29:11-13 (NIV)
*"For I know the plans I have for you," declares the Lord, "plans
to prosper you and not to harm you, plans to give you hope and
a future. Then you will call on me and come and pray to me, and
I will listen to you. You will seek me and find me when you seek
me with all your heart."* In order to have a successful business,
you must trust in the Lord. God's will is what is best for us.
There will be times when you do not understand why things are
happening in your business, but God is always trying to teach us
and protect us.
Isaiah 54:2-3 (NIV)
*Enlarge the place of your tent, stretch your tent curtains wide,
do not hold back; lengthen your cords, strengthen your stakes.
For you will spread out to the right and to the left; your
descendants will dispossess nations and settle in their desolate
cities.* You do not need to wait until you are rich and super-
successful to help others. You should help others now as you
are building your business. Now, that does not mean you should
go hungry to help others, but do not be afraid to enlarge your
tent to partner with "so called" competitors. There really is
enough business for everyone.

Showers Ink

NOTES

NOTES

NOTES

NOTES

NOTES

NOTES

NOTES

NOTES

NOTES

Thank You

Thank you for your time and support. I pray that this book has encouraged and given you your passion and drive to be and do everything God has created you for.

Until next time, stay prayerful, encouraged, and beautiful. May God increase and expand your business in ways you never imagined.

Sincerely,

Angela Showers

Angela Showers, LMT

Ordained Minister*Author*Certified
Christian Life Coach*Motivational
Speaker*Licensed Massage
Therapist*Entrepreneur

For Booking Info Visit:

www.BreathofLifeCoaching.com

* 9 7 8 1 4 9 0 9 1 9 6 2 1 *